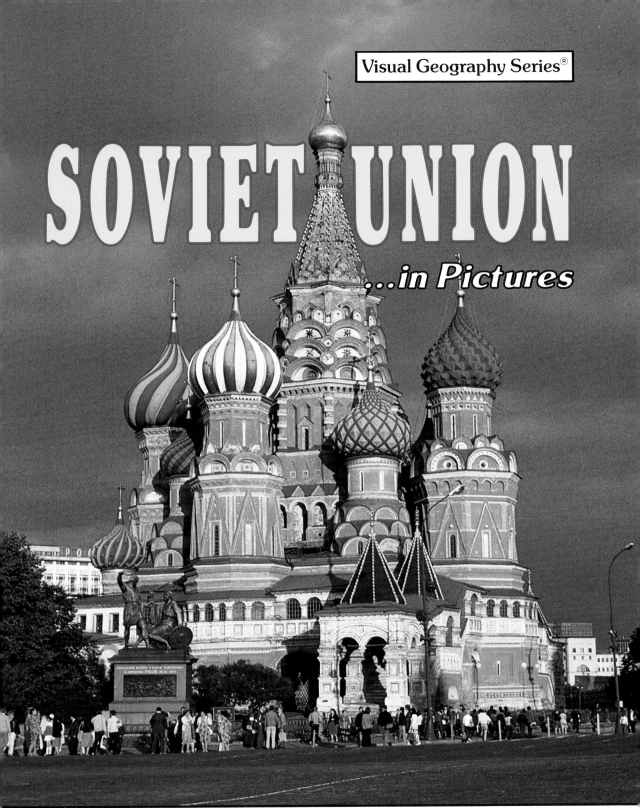

SOVIET UNION

...in Pictures

Prepared by
Stephen C. Feinstein

Lerner Publications Company
Minneapolis

Independent Picture Service

Children splash each other in a pool in Moscow, the Soviet Union's capital city.

PUBLISHER'S NOTE 1992

In the three years since this book was produced, many things have changed in the Soviet Union. In fact, the USSR we have known for 75 years no longer exists, and what will be in its place is far from certain.

Until the situation in the region settles down, we believe *Soviet Union in Pictures* can serve as a resource for understanding the past—a past that helped to create present conditions. We want to assure our readers, however, that we will update this edition in the near future.

LIBRARY OF CONGRESS CATALOGING-IN-PUBLICATION DATA

Feinstein, Steve.
    Soviet Union in pictures / prepared by Steve Feinstein.
    p. cm.—(Visual geography series)
    Rev. ed. of: Russia in pictures / prepared by Galina Klimenko.
    Includes index.
    Summary: The Soviet Union's topography, history, society, economy, and government are concisely described, augmented by photographs, maps, charts, and captions.
    ISBN 0-8225-1864-3 (lib. bdg.)
    1. Soviet Union. [1. Soviet Union.] I. Klimenko, Galina. Russia in pictures. II. Title. III. Series: Visual geography series (Minneapolis, Minn.)
DK17.F45   1989
947—dc19   88-37508
                                                CIP
                                                 AC

International Standard Book Number: 0-8225-1864-3
Library of Congress Catalog Card Number: 88-37508

VISUAL GEOGRAPHY SERIES®

Publisher
Harry Jonas Lerner
Associate Publisher
Nancy M. Campbell
Senior Editor
Mary M. Rodgers
Editors
Gretchen Bratvold
Dan Filbin
Photo Researcher
Karen A. Sirvaitis
Editorial/Photo Assistant
Marybeth Campbell
Consultants/Contributors
Stephen C. Feinstein
Sergey Chernyaev
Sandra K. Davis
Designer
Jim Simondet
Cartographer
Carol F. Barrett
Indexers
Kristine S. Schubert
Sylvia Timian
Production Manager
Gary J. Hansen

Courtesy of Rufina Chernyaev

After a long trek in the Caucasus Mountains, three Soviet youths relax in the snow.

This book is an all-new edition in the Visual Geography Series. Previous editions were published by Sterling Publishing Company, New York City. The text, set in 10/12 Century Textbook, is fully revised and updated, and new photogaphs, maps, charts, and captions have been added.

Acknowledgments

Title page photo courtesy of Russell Adams.

Elevation contours adapted from *The Times Atlas of the World*, seventh comprehensive edition (New York: Times Books, 1985).

3 4 5 6 7 8 9 10 99 98 97 96 95 94 93 92

In the Soviet republic of Turkmenistan, workers lay out hundreds of lamb skins to dry in the sun. (See page 45 for a map of the Soviet republics.)

Contents

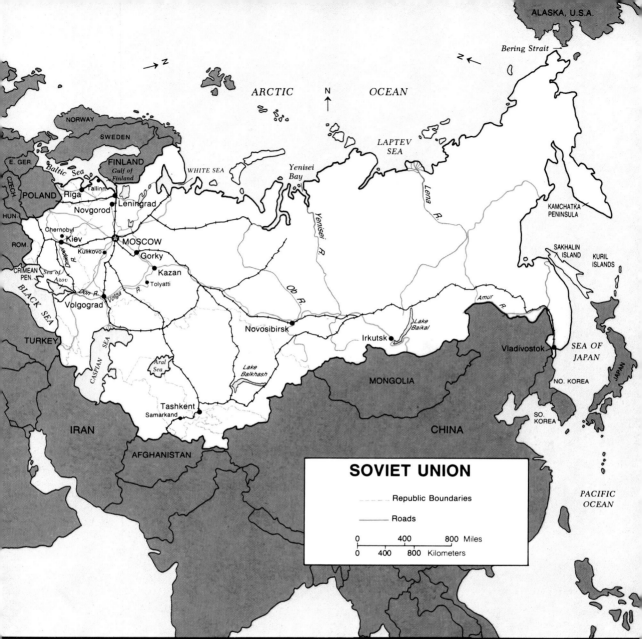

METRIC CONVERSION CHART
To Find Approximate Equivalents

WHEN YOU KNOW:	MULTIPLY BY:	TO FIND:
AREA		
acres	0.41	hectares
square miles	2.59	square kilometers
CAPACITY		
gallons	3.79	liters
LENGTH		
feet	30.48	centimeters
yards	0.91	meters
miles	1.61	kilometers
MASS (weight)		
pounds	0.45	kilograms
tons	0.91	metric tons
VOLUME		
cubic yards	0.77	cubic meters
TEMPERATURE		
degrees Fahrenheit	0.56 (*after* subtracting 32)	degrees Celsius

Courtesy of Steve Feinstein

Destroyed by an earthquake in 1966, the ancient city of Tashkent in the southwestern Soviet Union has been substantially rebuilt. The capital of the republic of Uzbekistan, Tashkent exhibits a harmonious blending of modern and Islamic styles.

Introduction

The Soviet Union, or the Union of Soviet Socialist Republics (USSR), covers vast areas of the European and Asian continents. In 1917 the Russian Revolution occurred, and it ushered in a Communist system of government. This event led to the establishment of the Soviet Union. Until 1922, the country was called Russia, because it included the land that comprised the early Russian states and the later Russian Empire.

The largest country on earth, the Soviet Union contains many ethnic groups. The nation's rich culture consists of both European and Asian peoples, whose ancestors have resided on the country's vast plains for centuries.

Foreign leaders saw the nation's flat landscape as an opportunity to invade. As a result, Scandinavian, Mongol, French, and German armies entered the region beginning in the ninth century. Sometimes

5

the newcomers intermarried with the local inhabitants. At other times, harsh winters and the resistance of the Russian (and later the Soviet) people destroyed the invaders' hopes of conquest.

Since World War II (1939–1945), the Soviet Union has been a world power, rivaling the United States in weaponry and scientific advances. Yet Soviet citizens often stand in long lines to buy food. Soviet strength has dominated the countries of Eastern Europe. But, within its own borders, the USSR has failed to produce enough consumer goods.

A new generation of Soviet leaders is attempting to solve these problems. Mikhail Gorbachev has led the country since 1985, and his goals include greater industrial and agricultural production. He has also encouraged openness—called *glasnost* in the Russian language—in areas that the government has long censored. Although the aims of the new regime seem promising, it is still unclear whether Gorbachev can motivate the Soviet people—and the sluggish Soviet bureaucracy—to achieve them.

In the city of Kiev, a streetside poster criticizes U.S. nuclear policy. Tension between the Soviet and U.S. governments increased after World War II (1939–1945), when the two nations began to compete for international influence.

Soviet citizens wait in a long line at a store in Leningrad. Much of a Soviet's average day can be spent searching for dwindling supplies of basic necessities, such as soap, sugar, and toilet paper.

In Siberia—a vast section of the Soviet Union that covers five million square miles—reindeer search for food in the snow.

1) The Land

As the largest country in the world, the Soviet Union covers about 8.6 million square miles. It is more than twice as big as the United States, including Hawaii and Alaska. Soviet territory takes up more than one-seventh of the earth's land. About one-fourth of the USSR is considered to be in Europe (a section called Soviet Europe), and the remainder lies in Asia.

The Soviet Union consists of 15 republics, the biggest of which is the Russian Soviet Federated Socialist Republic. (See the map on page 45.) With 76 percent of the nation's total area, the Russian republic covers huge sections of Europe and Asia. Dominating this republic is Siberia, a region of more than five million square miles that stretches from Soviet Europe to the Pacific Ocean.

Twelve countries border the USSR. To the northwest and west are Norway, Finland, Poland, Czechoslovakia, Hungary, and Romania. Along the Soviet Union's southern boundary are Turkey, Iran, Afghanistan, China, Mongolia, and North Korea. The USSR's northern and eastern coasts lie on inlets of the Arctic and Pacific oceans, respectively. In the far northeast, the 52-mile-wide Bering Strait separates the Soviet Union from Alaska.

Topography

Although the Soviet Union covers a vast area, it can be divided geographically into three general regions. A huge, low plain stretches eastward from Soviet Europe to the Yenisei River in central Asia. In the northeastern Soviet Union, the immense, elevated Central Siberian Plateau dominates the landscape and meets a section of uplands farther east. Along the USSR's southern frontier are mountain chains of varying heights that separate the Soviet Union from neighboring countries. Within these three broad regions—the flat western plain, the elevated northeastern plateau, and the southern string of mountains—are many smaller landforms.

WESTERN PLAIN

The western plain is a vast flatland whose average elevation rarely exceeds 600 feet above sea level. It includes three

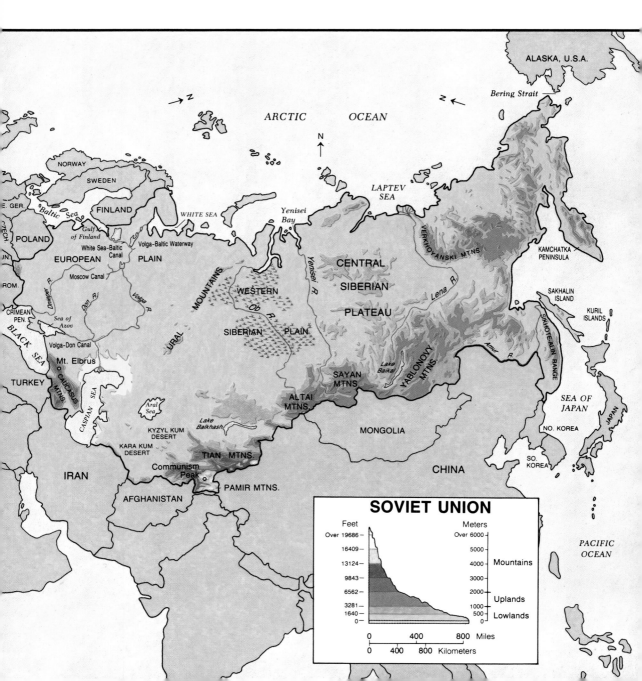

Within Alma-Ata—a political subunit of the Kazakh republic—the rugged Tian Mountains rise in terraces. Some of these peaks are always snow-capped, and even in summer the region experiences harsh temperatures.

subregions—the European Plain, the Ural Mountains, and the Western Siberian Plain. In the northwest is the European Plain, where about three-fourths of the Soviet Union's people live. The area's rich soil makes it agriculturally productive, and many of the USSR's factories are located in this part of Soviet Europe.

East of the plain are the Ural Mountains, a low range that has been worn down by streams. Traditionally, the Urals have divided the European and Asian parts of the Soviet Union. The range's average elevation is about 3,000 feet above sea level, with a few peaks that exceed 6,000 feet in height.

Beyond the Urals lies the Western Siberian Plain—a continuation of the immense flatland in the western Soviet Union. This plain alone covers more than one million square miles and rises no higher than 500 feet above sea level. The Western Siberian Plain is well watered but poorly drained, and it remains marshy or frozen most of the year.

CENTRAL SIBERIAN PLATEAU AND UPLANDS

The Central Siberian Plateau climbs to about 2,000 feet above sea level. Like the western plain, this area is huge, covering roughly 1.5 million square miles of ter-

ritory. Streams have cut deep canyons through the plateau, which is crossed by several ranges—including the Verkhoyanski Mountains—before it merges with the eastern uplands.

Mainly uninhabited and mountainous, the uplands of eastern Siberia reach 10,000 feet above sea level. High ranges also characterize the landscape of nearby Soviet islands and of the Kamchatka Peninsula, which includes several active volcanoes among its peaks.

SOUTHERN MOUNTAINS

A series of mountain ranges appears in the southern Soviet Union. In the southwest, the Caucasus Mountains rise to over 18,000 feet between the Caspian and Black seas. The range extends west to east for 700 miles. The highest point is Mount Elbrus, which, at 18,481 feet, is the tallest summit in Europe.

Southeastward, beyond the Kara Kum and Kyzyl Kum deserts, are the Pamir, Altai, and Tian mountains, which are among the world's highest ranges. The Soviet Union's tallest mountain—Communism Peak (24,590 feet)—rises within the Soviet Pamirs.

The Sayan Mountains are the first peaks in a string of lower elevations that

continues eastward to the Sikhote-Alin Range along the Sea of Japan. Between these two chains are the Yablonovy Mountains, which form a dividing point for rivers that flow north to the Arctic Ocean or east to the Pacific Ocean.

Rivers

The USSR has thousands of miles of navigable waterways. In the winter months, however, most of the rivers freeze and cannot be used for travel until spring.

The western Soviet Union contains the Volga and the Dnieper rivers. The Volga—Europe's longest waterway—flows for over 2,100 miles through the Russian republic until it empties into the Caspian Sea. The Volga is navigable for almost its entire course and has a fertile area at its mouth. Along the Volga's banks lie several Soviet cities, including Volgograd and Gorky.

A section of the Lena River—the Soviet Union's longest waterway—makes a wide sweep through the Yakutsk Autonomous Soviet Socialist Republic. This ethnic subunit of the Russian republic was set aside for the Yakut, a northeast Asian people who live in the Lena River Basin.

Fish thrive in the Volga, and its waters provide hydropower and irrigation.

The Dnieper begins near the source of the Volga River and travels for more than 1,400 miles through several Soviet republics to the Black Sea. Europe's third longest river, the Dnieper once formed the border between the Russian Empire and Poland. The waterway supplies hydroelectricity to the western Soviet Union.

Within the Western Siberian Plain flows the Ob River—a major transportation route in Siberia. Much of the Ob's course winds through swampland, yet the waterway has become an important hydroelectric power source in the central Soviet Union. Along the plain's frontier with the Central Siberian Plateau lies the Yenisei River. Its 2,566-mile-long circuit has many frozen stretches in the winter. The river cuts through mountains and plains to reach its Arctic outlet on Yenisei Bay.

The longest river completely within the Soviet Union is the Lena. Its 2,600-mile course begins in central Asia near Lake Baikal and travels northward through Siberia's woodlands before entering the Laptev Sea. The land bordering the river and its many tributaries is rich in minerals, including gold and diamonds.

Canals, which are used for both transportation and irrigation, connect many of the Soviet Union's major rivers. The most important links are the White Sea–Baltic Canal, the Moscow Canal, the Volga–Don Canal and the Volga–Baltic Waterway.

Seas and Lakes

Of primary importance to Soviet commerce is the Baltic Sea, which offers ships the shortest route to the Atlantic Ocean. The sea's shores border the republics of Latvia, Estonia, and Lithuania, which together are known as the Baltic States. The Caspian Sea—with an area of over 140,000 square miles—is the largest inland saltwater body in the world. Although several rivers, including the Volga, flow into the

A boat churns through the waters of the Black Sea along the coast of the Crimean Peninsula. Overlooking the scene is the Swallow's Nest, a castlelike structure that was built into the cliffs.

Twisted roots accent the landscape surrounding Lake Baikal, a long, narrow body of water in southern Siberia.

Caspian Sea, this body of water loses more of its volume from evaporation than it gains from incoming streams. As a result, the sea's surface area is shrinking.

The Soviet Union has several other inland bodies of water. Lake Baikal in southern Siberia fills the largest freshwater basin in Asia and Europe. The lake's maximum depth is over 5,700 feet, making it one of the deepest lakes in the world. Situated in the south central USSR is Lake Balkhash, a freshwater body that remains frozen from November to March. About 600 miles west of Lake Balkhash lies the salty Aral Sea, whose infertile shores are mostly uninhabited.

Climate

The wide expanse of the Soviet Union contains many climate zones, although winters are generally quite cold throughout the country. The western Soviet Union has short, dry summers and long, cold winters. Weather conditions in the European Plain are less severe than they are in areas east of the Urals. In winter, temperatures in the capital city of Moscow may drop to –10° F, and those in the northwestern city of Leningrad can dip to –35° F, but averages range from 15° to 30° F. Summer temperatures in these urban centers vary between 60° and 75° F.

Winter temperatures in the northeast often stay at about –5° F but occasionally fall to as low as –59° F. Intense blizzards bring strong winds mixed with snow, which blow over the enormous plains of the USSR. In the summer, on the other hand, the thermometers of south central Asia have registered temperatures of 120° F. Novosibirsk, the largest city in Siberia, averages –15° F in winter and about 75° F in summer.

Courtesy of Virginia Levy

In April a thin layer of snow covers an avenue in Leningrad. This city in the northwestern Soviet Union has average winter temperatures of about 17° F.

This pipeline in Siberia transports natural gas to populated regions of the Russian republic. The Soviet Union, or USSR, contains approximately 40 percent of the world's proven natural gas reserves.

The southwestern coastal regions have a subtropical climate similar to that of areas along the Mediterranean Sea, located farther west. Temperatures are milder in winter (usually above 30° F) and warmer in summer (about 90° F) than they are in much of the Soviet Union.

Both rain and snow descend on nearly all areas of the Soviet Union. As much as 100 inches of rain falls annually in the west, and Moscow and Leningrad each receive 20 to 30 inches per year. The central and eastern regions of the nation get much of their precipitation as snow. In the southern part of the USSR, the snow thaws in a month or two, while in the extreme northeast it may remain on the ground for nearly nine months.

Parts of the Soviet Union, particularly in the southwest, lie along cracks in the earth's surface. When the plates of land shift, earthquakes sometime occur. In December 1988, the Soviet republic of Armenia experienced a very destructive quake that killed thousands of people and left thousands of others homeless.

Natural Resources

The Soviet Union is nearly self-sufficient in natural resources. The USSR possesses about one-fifth of the world's forested land. Much of the western woodlands are logged for timber.

Huge reserves of copper and about half of the world's iron ore exist in the Soviet Union. The nation's coal resources are second only to those of the United States. Containing vast amounts of the world's oil, the USSR is also rich in reserves of natural gas. Other valuable minerals in the Soviet Union include silver, gold, diamonds, manganese, lead, zinc, salt, and nickel.

Flora and Fauna

The Soviet Union has three general vegetation zones. From north to south, these zones include the tundra, the forest, and the steppes (plains). The tundra, a permafrost (permanently frozen) area, stretches along the shores of the Arctic Ocean. Bleak and unforested, this frozen wasteland is sparsely dotted with patches of moss, as

Dense woodlands exist in many parts of the Soviet Union, especially in the east, where weather conditions prevent extensive logging operations.

well as occasional bushes and dwarf trees. The few shrubs capable of surviving the region's fierce winter climate grow in tangled clusters. The land becomes marshy and mosquito-infested in the short summer season.

Immediately south of the tundra, covering nearly half of the Soviet Union, sprawls a dense forest zone, or taiga. Almost every species of tree grows somewhere in this enormous area of over four million square miles. Southern regions of the taiga contain stands of silver birch, oak, maple, linden, and spruce.

A narrow section of land known as the forest steppe links the forests of the north and the steppes of the south. In this strip, thick stands of trees alternate with great open spaces. The steppes are vast, grassy expanses that offer good natural conditions for farming. Covered by a wide variety of feather grasses that are several feet tall, the steppes also contain flowers, such as tulips and hyacinths.

A thin coastal strip along the Black Sea —including the Crimean Peninsula—does not belong to the three general vegetation zones. The subtropical flora along this coast is unlike that of any other region of the country. The coastal hills are thick with plant life, and vines climb up rocky cliffs. The coastline features magnolia, eucalyptus, and hibiscus trees.

Polar bears, foxes, lemmings, and reindeer roam the icy, windswept tundra. The Soviet Union's vast forests abound with fur-bearing animals, including sables and mink, whose pelts are highly prized. Deer, brown bears, and wolves also roam the forests. In the far eastern areas live tigers, panthers, and snow leopards.

The tall grasses of the steppes provide homes for small animals, such as wild hamsters, marmots, and mice. Desert regions contain lizards, tortoises, snakes, gazelles, and antelope. Porcupines and wild boars live in the subtropics.

To keep warm in the Soviet winter, some animals burrow in the snow.

A pair of polar bears roam arctic areas of the USSR in search of food. The second largest bear species, polar bears have poor eyesight and hearing but possess an excellent sense of smell. Their diet often includes sea animals—fish, seals, and walrus, for example. Strong swimming abilities and powerful front paws enable the bears to catch their prey.

15

Cities

About two-thirds of the Soviet Union's people are urban dwellers. The nation has dozens of cities with over 500,000 inhabitants. Only three, however—Moscow, Leningrad, and Kiev—have more than two million residents, and all three are located in Soviet Europe.

MOSCOW

With 8.5 million people in its metropolitan area, Moscow is the USSR's largest city and one of its most historic urban centers. Founded in the twelfth century by a Russian prince, Moscow grew in succeeding centuries under the rule of the Mongols from central Asia. By the late 1400s, the Mongols had been overthrown, and Moscow became the capital of the Russian Empire, which was ruled by tsars (emperors).

In 1712 Tsar Peter I moved the capital from Moscow to his new city called St. Petersburg (now Leningrad), but Moscow remained a major cultural and trading center. After 1917, the Communist leadership reestablished Moscow as the Soviet Union's capital.

Many of Moscow's residents—who are called Muscovites—work in offices of the Communist party or the Soviet government. These workers must have the government's permission to live in the city—a rule designed to prevent urban overcrowding. Moscow is also a huge industrial hub with factories that produce vehicles, chemicals, tools, and textiles.

In the center of Moscow is the Kremlin, an old fortress from tsarist days that has become the headquarters of the Soviet government. Just outside the Kremlin lies Red Square—a large, open area whose

Courtesy of Russell Adams

Moscow's Red Square—with the onion-shaped domes of St. Basil's Cathedral at one end—attracts foreign tourists as well as Soviet citizens. Over 1,000 feet long, the square hosts annual parades and national celebrations. GUM—the country's large state department store—occupies one side of the plaza.

Midday shoppers crowd a street in Leningrad, a city built along the banks of the Neva River. Crisscrossed by canals and rising only a little above sea level, Leningrad is subject to flooding in spring, when the frozen Neva begins to thaw.

name comes from a Russian word that means both "beautiful" and "red." Surrounding Red Square are St. Basil's Cathedral, the Lenin Mausoleum (a tomb where the preserved body of Vladimir Ilich Lenin, the founder of the Soviet Union, is on display), and GUM—the nation's biggest department store.

LENINGRAD

About 4.8 million people live in Leningrad—the Soviet Union's second largest urban center. The Neva River flows through the city, making some parts of Leningrad marshy in the spring. But the waterway also leads to the Gulf of Finland, which is an arm of the strategic Baltic Sea.

For about two centuries, Leningrad was known as St. Petersburg. The city's ornate buildings housed the tsars (emperors) and their courts. The blue-and-white Hermitage Museum was originally part of the royal Winter Palace. Built between 1754 and 1762 for the Russian empress Elizabeth I, the Winter Palace was used for formal meetings and grand receptions. The building now contains an extensive collection of international artworks.

Leningrad's location has made it one of the USSR's major ports.

Founded as Russia's new capital city by Peter I, Leningrad (then called St. Petersburg) was designed to resemble the great cities of Western Europe. The tsar's architects built visual masterpieces, including royal palaces, magnificent churches, and broad public squares. Despite damage from wars and revolutions, Leningrad has retained much of its eighteenth-century grandeur.

Among the city's most famous landmarks are the Hermitage Museum and the Cathedral of St. Isaac of Dalmatia. The museum—which holds outstanding collections of Greek, Roman, Islamic, and European artworks—was originally the Winter Palace of the tsars. The cathedral's distinctive golden dome dominates Leningrad's skyline.

KIEV

Kiev—a city of 2.4 million people in the Ukrainian Soviet Socialist Republic—thrived long before Moscow and Leningrad were built. A settlement existed on the site in the A.D. 600s. In the late 800s,

Small, enclosed boats are a swift and reliable means of transport on Leningrad's river and canals.

Courtesy of Harlan V. Anderson

Built in the nineteenth century, the Cathedral of St. Isaac of Dalmatia is Leningrad's largest church. Now a museum, the cathedral took 40 years to construct and includes marble-lined walls and a heavily gilded dome.

Courtesy of Steve Feinstein

Kiev, a flourishing center of one of Russia's earliest civilizations, lost many of its historic buildings in battles during World War II. St. Sophia's Cathedral *(center right)* — first erected in the eleventh century — remained standing.

Kiev became the capital of Kievan Russia —the first major Russian principality (realm of a prince). In the twelfth century, Kiev was a prosperous trading center, but the Mongols destroyed it a century later. At different times, Lithuania and Poland governed Kiev. After a series of wars in the 1600s, the Russian Empire reestablished its control over Kiev. Since then, the city has remained within Russian or Soviet territory.

Because of its long history, Kiev has many significant buildings, including ancient monasteries, St. Sophia's Cathedral, and the Marinsky Palace. Modern Kiev has developed a strong industrial base, and its factories manufacture airplanes, clothing, tools, cameras, and watches.

19

The USSR adopted this version of its flag in 1955. The hammer and sickle—which represent urban and rural workers, respectively—have become symbolic of international Communism. Many other Communist countries now use these tools on their emblems. The five-pointed star stands for the unity of Communist workers on five continents, and the color red represents the revolution.

2) History and Government

Humans from the successive Stone, Copper, and Bronze ages inhabited the Soviet Union thousands of years ago. Most of these people, who led a nomadic lifestyle, lived in the western part of the country. When humans discovered iron in about 1000 B.C., an Asian people called Cimmerians dwelt along the shores of the Black Sea. By the seventh century B.C., a central Asian group known as the Scythians had conquered the Cimmerians.

The Scythians developed a diverse culture that produced richly decorated weapons, jewelry, and household items. The Scythians also had trade and military contacts with Greece and Persia (modern Iran). A gradual decline of the Scythian Empire enabled the Sarmatians from central Asia to take control of the area in the third century B.C. Like the Scythian Empire, the Sarmatian state was a loosely organized grouping of strong clans. This political system—as well as a highly efficient military force—controlled the region from the Volga to the Danube (a river in central Europe) until the A.D. 200s.

Early Invaders

Attracted by the fertile steppes, Germanic Goths destroyed Sarmatian rule around the Black Sea in the mid-third century A.D. But by the late fourth century, the Huns—another central Asian people—had defeated the Goths. The Goths fled westward, and the Huns established themselves around the Black Sea. The skilled Hun troops conquered many neighboring groups under their khan (leader) Attila, but after Attila's death in 453, the Hun Empire faltered.

The Avars, a nomadic people from central Asia, took over a portion of the Hun lands in 560. They made repeated attempts to expand their territory but failed in a succession of bloody battles. By the seventh century, the Khazar people controlled much of the region around central Asia, the Caucasus Mountains, and the Volga River.

THE EASTERN SLAVS

Throughout the period of these rising and falling realms, large numbers of central Asians were moving westward. They eventually populated the nations that now make up Eastern Europe. In time, these peoples came to be called Slavs and separated into southern, western, and eastern subgroups. The southern and western Slavs are the ancestors of today's Yugoslavians, Czechoslovakians, Poles, and Bulgarians. The eastern Slavs inhabited the present-day Soviet republics of Byelorussia, Russia, and the Ukraine. Many historians believe that the word *Russia* came from *Rus*, the name of one of the Slavic subgroups.

Although the eastern Slavs were strong in number, they were plagued by invasions from neighboring nomadic groups. By the ninth century, the eastern Slavs had established themselves in what is now Soviet

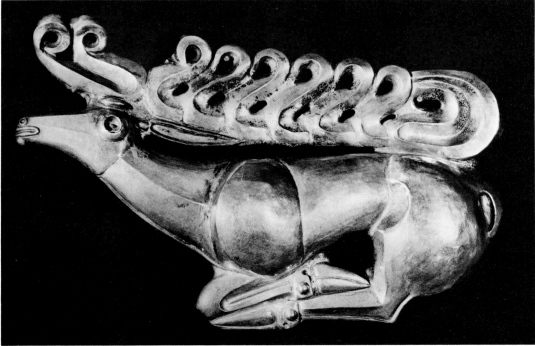

Scythian artisans created a variety of practical and decorative items, including this gold medallion dating from the sixth century B.C. The Scythians dominated the region around the Black Sea between the seventh and third centuries B.C.

Europe—notably in the trading cities of Novgorod in the northeast and Kiev in the southwest. But the Slavs were not a unified people and often quarreled among themselves. According to the *Primary Chronicle*—an early written account of Russian history—the disunity of the Slavs enabled soldiers from Scandinavia to take control of Slavic lands. The conquerors were called the Varangians.

By 862 the Varangian leader Rurik had taken control of Novgorod. His successor, Oleg, captured Kiev in 882 and moved his government to this southwestern city. Oleg—the first prince of Kievan Russia—developed the city into a flourishing commercial and cultural center.

Kievan Russia

By the tenth century, many other principalities besides Kievan Russia had arisen in western areas of the present-day Soviet Union. The person who reigned over Kiev was called a grand prince, however, and he had greater power than the other princes.

Kiev was a crossroads for important trade routes. Commercial ventures brought Kievan Russia into frequent contact with the Byzantine Empire, whose capital—Constantinople—was located in what is now Turkey. As a result of their commercial ties, Constantinople influenced Kievan Russia in many ways.

In A.D. 988, Grand Prince Vladimir spearheaded a major change in Russian society. He accepted the Orthodox form of Christianity, which was followed in Constantinople, and made it the state religion. Eventually, the religious organization in Russia came to be called the Russian Orthodox Church. The religion's leaders influenced Russian life and culture. Russian builders developed a local architectural style that echoed Byzantine forms, and Russian artists painted beautiful icons (religious portraits).

Courtesy of Steve Feinstein

Grand Prince Yaroslav dedicated St. Sophia's Cathedral in 1037, about 50 years after Kievan Russia formally adopted Christianity. Yaroslav, who promoted the religion's acceptance among his subjects, is buried in the cathedral's northeastern corner.

The decline of Kievan Russia began in the eleventh century, when Grand Prince Yaroslav ordered his realm to be divided among his sons after his death. This move weakened the state and allowed princes in other cities to compete with Kiev for power.

Kiev's final downfall came with the invasion of the Mongols in the 1220s. With the skillful use of warriors on horseback, this group of central Asians had been expanding their territory for several decades. Led by Genghis Khan, the Mongols attacked the Russian steppes in 1223 but did not fully subdue the area. Genghis's grandson Batu Khan renewed the fight in 1237. The invaders massacred more than half the population and enslaved those that remained alive. Kiev was destroyed in 1240. By the mid-thirteenth century, Kievan Russia was in Mongol hands.

Mongol Rule

Batu Khan established the khanate (empire) of the Golden Horde in southern and western Russia. For over 200 years, Mongol rule shaped Russian life. The conquerors periodically attacked and destroyed entire communities. Yet the Mongols chose to use local leaders, instead of their own administrators, to run the new territories. As a result, many Russian princes served in the Mongol government. The Mongols demanded tribute—payment of taxes—from all of the principalities under their authority.

The two centuries of Mongol control isolated the Russians from other cultures. Industry and the arts made little progress, and Mongol laws and customs influenced traditional forms of government. The Russian language adopted many words from the Mongolian tongue, and Mongol styles of clothing remained popular in Russia even after Mongol rule ended.

Yet Mongol control did not wipe out the Russian system of principalities. Vladimir, one of the most important principalities,

Independent Picture Service

The Mongol chief Batu Khan conquered Kievan Russia, as well as what is now Kazakhstan, in the late 1230s. His empire, or khanate, was called the Golden Horde, after the color of his tent and the word *orda,* meaning "camp." Europeans referred to the Mongols, who originally came from Mongolia in eastern Asia, as Tartars. The name is a mistaken version of Tatar, which the Mongols used to identify themselves.

was located near the Volga River and included the dukedom of Moscow. Mongol khans favored rulers from this dukedom because it was located along major trade routes. With Mongol support, the dukes of Moscow enlarged their territory by absorbing surrounding lands. By 1301 Moscow had become a separate principality.

The influence of the Muscovite leaders increased steadily in the fourteenth century. One of them persuaded the head of the Russian Orthodox Church to move from Kiev to Moscow. This change—as well as the wealth and loyalty of the local

The Battle of Kulikovo—in which Russian troops defeated Mongol forces —was a turning point in Mongol control of Russia. Fought in 1380 near the Don River, the battle proved that the foreign rulers could be beaten. A century later, the Mongols no longer had authority over Russia.

boyars (large landowners)—increased Moscow's importance.

Struggles among the leaders of the Golden Horde weakened the Mongol Empire, enabling Russian power to reemerge. In 1380, at the Battle of Kulikovo, the Muscovite leader Dmitry defeated a Mongol army. In 1480 another Muscovite prince, Ivan III, refused to pay tribute to the Golden Horde. These events demonstrated the inability of the Mongols to discipline their territories, and foreign rule soon disintegrated.

The First Tsars

After Ivan III (called the Great) added the principalities of Novgorod and Tver to his lands, he considered himself tsar (emperor, also spelled czar) of all Russia. Under Ivan, Moscow became a capital city, with beautiful churches and magnificent palaces. Ivan's successors in the sixteenth century put their energy into uniting their expanding territory under one rule.

Ivan III, also called Ivan the Great, was the ruler of the principality of Moscow. He inherited his lands in 1462. By the time of his death in 1505, he had substantially expanded his realm. Ivan's territorial gains formed the foundation of the Russian Empire.

Although the realm grew in size, it was difficult to control, mainly because the boyars were trying to seize more land and power for themselves. The ruler of Moscow at this time was Ivan IV, who had become tsar in 1533 at the age of three. When allowed to reign without supervision in 1547, he took action against the boyars. Members of Ivan's personal police force killed landowners who opposed the tsar and seized their estates.

During Ivan's reign, areas around the Volga River came under Russian authority, and Russian troops conquered Siberia. Ivan IV earned the name "the Terrible" because of his violent temper and his preference for brutal forms of punishment.

Ivan IV wanted to increase the prestige of his realm. He initiated closer contact with Europe, which improved economic conditions as technical experts from other countries helped Russia to modernize. The tsar also founded the Zemsky Sobor, a national assembly of loyal landowners that met at the tsar's whim.

SERFS AND TROUBLES

Before the sixteenth century, members of the Russian peasantry were allowed to travel freely, which they usually did after the harvest season was over. At the end of the sixteenth century, however, growing numbers of peasants were avoiding taxes and military service by fleeing to

The rise of Moscow's political fortunes in the fifteenth century brought architectural changes to the city. Within its Kremlin, or fort, artisans constructed churches and palaces. The Cathedral of the Assumption, designed in the 1470s by an Italian architect, became the center of royal ceremonies.

regions on the nation's borders. As a result, the government gradually restricted the right of the peasants to relocate.

Although neither serfs nor slaves had personal freedom or physical mobility, serfdom was different from slavery in important ways. Serfs could not be removed from the land on which they worked. Harshly treated by the landowners, the serfs frequently rebelled. When the rural unrest spread, it unsettled the central government.

Adding to these concerns was the failure of Ivan IV's successor, Fyodor, to provide an heir. Fyodor died in 1598, and his brother Dmitry was secretly murdered. The appearance of several "False Dmitries" (royal imposters) weakened the government. This period, called the "Time of Troubles," lasted until 1613. In that year, the Zemsky Sobor elected Michael Romanov, a cousin of Ivan IV, to be tsar. Michael founded the Romanov dynasty (family of rulers), which governed Russia for more than 300 years.

Under the first few Romanov tsars, the government increased the power of the landowners over the serfs. In 1649, for example, the Zemsky Sobor established serfdom as a legal institution protected by

A typical peasant dwelling consisted of one large room that had neither a chimney nor windows. In the winter, the family shared its living space with its livestock. Some family members slept on top of the brick oven to keep warm. Most serfs were illiterate, unskilled, underfed, and overworked.

Independent Picture Service

The Zemsky Sobor, or Assembly of Landowners, elected Michael Romanov to be tsar in 1613. Here, religious leaders escort the tsar into the Cathedral of the Assumption to be crowned.

Photo by Bettmann Archive

The Bronze Horseman—an equestrian statue of Peter the Great—stands on a pedestal in a Leningrad square. Born in Moscow in 1672, Peter became tsar at the age of 10 along with his older half brother Ivan V. In 1696 Ivan died, and Peter assumed complete control of Russian affairs. Soon afterward, Peter traveled throughout Europe, coaxing technicians and scholars to come to Russia to help him bring the empire into the modern era. Possessing both great energy and a fiery temper, Peter devoted himself to improving his realm's military capabilities and to Westernizing his subjects. St. Petersburg (now Leningrad)—his port on the Baltic Sea—became a center of shipbuilding, culture, and architectural splendor. Some of Peter's changes angered members of the nobility—including the tsar's son and heir Alexis, who was condemned to death for opposing his father's reforms. When Peter died in 1725, Russia had a strong army and navy, a large number of foreign advisers, and a more Western outlook.

Courtesy of Russell Adams

Russian law. Many serfs fled to remote areas of the empire to escape lives of hardship and domination. In 1670 some of these serfs, led by Stenka Razin, revolted against landowners in southeastern Russia. Tsarist troops put down the uprising. The early Romanovs also faced serious financial difficulties caused by the frequent bankruptcy of the Russian treasury. Further problems resulted when Sweden and Poland attacked Russia's borders.

These difficulties led to a power struggle when Tsar Fyodor III died in 1682. The political factions could not agree on a successor. Therefore, two young half brothers —Ivan V and Peter I—were chosen to share the throne. Ivan V died in 1696, and, at the age of 24, Peter I took full charge of Russian affairs.

Peter I and Catherine II

An admirer of Western European ideas, Peter I (called the Great) forced a series of reforms on his subjects. He introduced new industries, created a regular army and navy, and reorganized state ministries. He put the Russian Orthodox Church under his direct rule, revised the nation's financial system, and made education compulsory for children of the nobility. Peter also forced aristocrats to dress in the European

A period cartoon depicts one of Peter's most visible changes—forcing Russian men to cut off their beards. He also altered the clothing styles worn in Russia.

way—a change that required noblemen to shorten their robes and shave their beards.

In 1703, to symbolize the beginning of a new European era for the empire, Peter began the construction of St. Petersburg on the Gulf of Finland. In 1712 he made the city the new capital of Russia. Seeking access to the Baltic Sea, Peter had acquired the regions of Estonia, Livonia, and Finland by 1721, after 20 years of fighting against Sweden.

Peter's reforms did not affect the serfs, however. Under his rule, they became more bound to the soil than they had been under previous tsars. Nor did Peter enact any changes that might limit his power. In his view, Russia could advance only under an autocrat—a ruler with unlimited authority.

The tsars who followed Peter were weak, and they involved Russia in several wars against the Germans and the Turks. In the Seven Years' War of the mid-eighteenth century, Elizabeth I of Russia allied her empire against Prussia (a region now di-

vided among Germany, Poland, and the USSR). Just as Prussia's defeat seemed certain, Elizabeth died. Her successor, Peter III, admired the ruler of Prussia and withdrew Russia from the conflict in 1762. This abrupt change of policy angered many Russians, and Peter III was assassinated later that year. His death brought his German-born wife, Catherine II (called the Great), to the tsarist throne.

Catherine II followed Peter the Great's policy of expanding Russia's territories. She added parts of Poland, Byelorussia, and the Ukraine to the empire's holdings. Under Catherine, Russian art and culture flourished. Although she talked about political and social reforms, her laws maintained royal power.

Just outside St. Petersburg, Peter ordered a country residence, Peterhof (now in a suburb called Petrodvorets), to be built. Severely damaged in the 1940s, the grounds and palaces have been painstakingly restored. The Great Cascade consists of three waterfalls and dozens of fountains and statues.

The Growth of Russia, 1533-1801

NORTH SEA

BALTIC SEA

BARENTS SEA

Novaya Zemlya

White Sea

ARCTIC OCEAN

BERING SEA

Dnieper R.

St. Petersburg

Moscow

S I B E R I A

KAMCHATKA PENINSULA

Lena River

Volga River

Ob River

Yenisei River

Yakutsk

SEA OF OKHOTSK

Black Sea

Aral Sea

Lake Baikal

Caspian Sea

SEA OF JAPAN

Areas Acquired

Before 1533	1598-1725
1533-1598	1725-1801

Between the sixteenth and eighteenth centuries, the Russian Empire expanded its borders. The early tsars acquired the vast Asian lands of Siberia, and later rulers took over parts of eastern Europe.

During Catherine's reign, the privileged classes benefited, but the oppression of the serfs continued. Another serf uprising occurred in 1773 and engulfed the empire from the Ural Mountains to the Volga River. Government troops defeated the rebels in 1774. Fearful of widespread discontent, Catherine strengthened the government's authority with the help of the army.

Catherine II, also called Catherine the Great, was not Russian but German. Although she had no legal right to rule the Russian Empire, Catherine succeeded her husband, Tsar Peter III, in 1762 at the age of 33. Her interest in art, literature, and science encouraged a large creative output during her reign. She fostered education for women and promoted better health practices. Nevertheless, her extravagant lifestyle, which included a long succession of royal romances, nearly overshadowed her attempts at administrative reform.

Seated on a black stallion, the rebel leader Yemelyan Pugachov greets some of his followers during the peasant revolt of 1773-1774. Pugachov's aim was to overthrow Catherine II, and he promised his supporters freedom from the rule of landowners. The rebellion's spectacular success unnerved wealthy Russians, and government troops finally subdued Pugachov's forces. The rebel leader was taken to Moscow in an iron cage and beheaded in 1775.

The 1800s

Under Alexander I, Catherine's eventual successor, Russia fought one of its most important wars, repelling the French army of Napoleon Bonaparte. Seeking to force Russia to close its ports to British trade, Napoleon invaded with 600,000 soldiers in 1812. The Russians retreated from the advancing French army. They burned their own land and cities—including Moscow—

In 1803 the Isaakievsky Bridge in St. Petersburg was decorated to celebrate the 100th anniversary of the founding of the city.

to deny the invaders food and housing as they made their way across Russia.

Faced with this "scorched earth" policy and unable to feed or shelter his troops in the harsh winter, Napoleon was forced to withdraw. After Napoleon's final defeat at Waterloo, Belgium, in 1815, the Congress of Vienna confirmed Russia as one of the leading powers of Europe.

Meanwhile, young Russian nobles had absorbed some of the new political ideals —such as personal liberty and social equality—that had become popular in Europe in the early 1800s. Many of the young aristocrats became members of secret organizations that sought to overthrow the autocracy. This form of government gave the tsar unlimited power. The young activists wanted to make Russia a constitutional monarchy with a written constitution that would limit the tsar's authority.

In December 1825, when Alexander I died and Nicholas I became tsar, the revolutionary aristocrats—called Decembrists —rebelled. A confrontation between the Decembrists and government troops in St. Petersburg ended when the soldiers fired canons at the demonstrators.

Courtesy of Library of Congress

Tsar Alexander II succeeded his father to the throne in 1855. As heir, Alexander had traveled throughout the empire to study its problems. One of his early measures as tsar was to free the serfs—a reform that affected four-fifths of the Russian population. Other changes improved the school and court systems. Many activists believed the reforms were too slow and limited. These discontented Russians formed terrorist groups, and one group-member assassinated Alexander II in 1881.

WAR AND REFORM

In addition to its internal problems, Russia was involved in international conflicts. In the mid-nineteenth century, Nicholas I led Russia into a war against the Turks that was fought on the Crimean Peninsula. Russia's defeat in the Crimean War (1854–1855) cost Russia some territories that it had previously gained from the Turks.

Nicholas I died during the Crimean conflict, and Alexander II succeeded him. The new tsar improved the educational and judicial systems, reorganized the army, relaxed censorship laws, and supported some self-government at the local level. Alexander's most important reform occurred in 1861, when he abolished serfdom. Yet this decree did not immediately improve the status of the peasants because they had to purchase their land and freedom from the landowners. The payments were large, and the peasants remained poor. Many landowners feared that the change would ruin Russia's economy, which survived on the taxes and labor of serfs.

Initially, Alexander's reforms raised the hopes of the impoverished majority for a better standard of living. Many people were disappointed when the reforms progressed slowly. In the 1870s, groups of revolutionaries staged hundreds of local demonstrations in support of more and faster changes. Because of these rallies, the government rapidly returned to strict policies, including censorship. The restrictions caused more unrest. Amid these troubles, a terrorist assassinated Alexander II in 1881 in St. Petersburg.

31

The coat of arms of the tsars featured a double eagle, which Ivan the Great adopted in the late fifteenth century to suggest Russia's growing strength. Peter I added the naval maps clutched in the beak and talons of each of the eagles. The emblem was used until the fall of the Romanov dynasty in 1917.

Artwork by Laura Westlund

Alexander III succeeded his father and sought to increase the tsar's authority. He further restricted freedom of the press and reduced local self-government. He also strengthened the power of landowners over peasants. Despite having been freed, peasants still lived under the control of the landowners. In 1894 Alexander died and left the throne to his 26-year-old son, Nicholas.

Nicholas II and the Marxists

Young, naive, and inexperienced, Nicholas II was easily influenced by ambitious advisers. Like other tsars before him, he believed his royal powers were unlimited. Russia's interests in China led Nicholas to engage in an unpopular war against Japan between 1904 and 1905. Defeat in that war strengthened the revolutionary movement, which took advantage of general dissatisfaction within Russia among urban and rural workers.

On Sunday, January 9, 1905, a crowd of dissatisfied laborers gathered in the streets of St. Petersburg. Carrying religious icons and pictures of Nicholas II, they marched to the tsar's palace to ask him to improve working conditions. When the crowd refused to leave, royal guards fired on the demonstrators, killing more than 130 of them and wounding several hundred others.

A wave of riots, strikes, murders, and rural revolts followed this event, which came to be known as Bloody Sunday. The general unrest forced Nicholas II to agree to the October Manifesto. This decree established a limited constitution, with a duma (legislature) whose members would be democratically elected. Following the manifesto, many political parties formed, including some that supported parliamentary government and several that promoted revolution.

Some of the revolutionaries called themselves Marxists because they followed the ideas of the nineteenth-century German writer Karl Marx. They believed that economic conditions shaped human institutions and that history was a series of struggles between the wealthy and the poor. Eventually, the Marxists formed the Russian Social Democratic Labor party, which divided into two subgroups—the Bolsheviks and the Mensheviks.

One of Marxism's supporters in Russia was Vladimir Ilich Lenin. His Bolsheviks urged working people to seize power and to use it for their own benefit. These Marxists wanted to eliminate the monarchy and to establish a republic based on socialist principles, which included shared landownership and equal distribution of income and goods.

World War I

While new ideas and political changes developed within Russia, the empire continued to fulfill its international obligations.

Independent Picture Service

With his arms raised, Father George Gapon—leader of the 1905 demonstration of striking workers—gestures to the tsar's troops on Bloody Sunday. Hoping to present their grievances to Tsar Nicholas II, the strikers ignored warnings to leave. The troops fired at the crowd, killing over 100 people and wounding many others.

Russia became a member of the Triple Entente—a three-part alliance with Great Britain and France—which was designed to curb German expansion. This agreement went into effect when Russia went to war against Germany at the start of World War I (1914–1918).

Russia experienced defeat and hardship during the war. The German army overran the Russian troops, who had neither adequate supplies nor skilled military leadership. Thousands of soldiers deserted the army, and many Russians did not support the global conflict.

In addition to Russia's wartime problems, the tsar's wife—Tsarina Alexandra—brought a new influence into the royal household. The tsarina believed that Grigory Rasputin, a self-styled holy man, could control her son's hemophilia (a life-threatening blood disease). As a result of Alexandra's confidence in him, Rasputin wielded great power. Through Alexandra, he advised the tsar on military and governmental matters. To eliminate Rasputin's influence, several nobles conspired to assassinate him in 1916. Following Rasputin's death, Nicholas seemed even less able to rule.

Meanwhile, soldiers as well as city workers lacked food, fuel, and adequate housing. Government ministries did not respond to the people's demands for coal and bread. In March 1917, riots broke out in Moscow and Petrograd (St. Petersburg's new, non-German name), and the tsar ordered his troops to stop the protesters. But instead of battling the rioters, the soldiers joined them. The Duma forced Nicholas II to give up his throne and organized a provisional (temporary) government.

In November 1917—before the provisional regime had stabilized—Lenin's Bolsheviks seized the government. They set up a dictatorship of the workers, and all land was nationalized (changed from private to government ownership). The Bolsheviks concluded a peace treaty with the Germans at Brest Litovsk in March

In June 1917, soon after Nicholas II had given up his throne, soldiers and workers marched in Petrograd (the Russian name for St. Petersburg). The participants were protesting the temporary government's efforts to continue fighting in World War I.

1918. Lenin moved the government back to Moscow in 1918 and renamed his political organization the Communist party. His regime marked the first time that governmental authority was organized along Communist and socialist ideals.

The Soviet Union

For the next two years, Russia endured a bloody civil war. The White Russians—anti-Communists who were aided by Western nations—clashed with the Bolsheviks throughout Russia. The Bolsheviks, however, emerged as the victors in 1920. By 1922 Russia had control over the soviets, or councils, of the neighboring Ukrainian, Byelorussian, and Transcaucasian republics. Together, these states formed the Union of Soviet Socialist Republics.

The Soviet Union emerged from its civil war in a state of economic collapse. The badly managed industrial sector produced few consumer goods, and agricultural output was below prewar levels. As a result of these problems, the government nationalized all industries and seized agricultural harvests. A drought in 1920 and 1921 led to a nationwide famine, in which five million people died.

Overwhelmed by problems, the government consolidated its power in the 1920s. Lenin introduced the New Economic Policy (NEP), which allowed small, independent businesses to operate and which permitted farmers to keep part of their harvest. To some degree, this policy improved economic conditions.

A fierce power struggle erupted when Lenin died in 1924. The chief rivals were Josef Stalin, Nikolai Bukharin, and Leon Trotsky—longtime colleagues of Lenin. Stalin won political control and extended a rigid dictatorship throughout the Soviet Union.

Stalin's Era

Stalin abandoned the NEP in 1928 and introduced the first five-year plan—an economic program that focused on specific national goals over a five-year period. He also helped the government gradually to gain control over most aspects of Soviet life, including politics, culture, education, and public information.

Stalin again forced farmers to give most of their harvest to the government. When they objected, he sent the farmers and their families to prison labor camps in

Siberia. In the 1930s, as both ordinary and highly placed Soviet citizens opposed Stalin's programs, he punished or killed millions of workers, military leaders, and political opponents. The government encouraged members of families to inform on their relatives' activities. It held false trials in which the accused people were forced to confess to crimes against the regime. In this way, Stalin removed his opponents and critics. The government also heavily censored public information so that the extent of Stalin's oppression was not widely known.

THE GREAT PATRIOTIC WAR

The Soviet Union had established a political system unlike any other in the world. In the 1930s, its leaders believed that outside powers threatened the nation's economic and political stability and that the wisest course was to avoid conflicts with strong foreign powers. As a result, the Soviet Union concluded a non-aggression pact with Germany in 1939, under which the Soviets and the Germans agreed not to attack each other.

The pact occurred when the warlike movements of Adolf Hitler, Germany's leader,

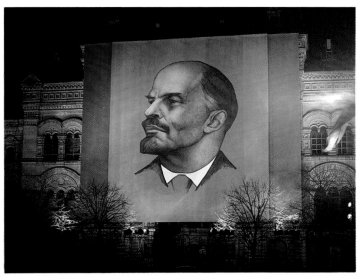

A huge banner carries the image of Vladimir Ilich Lenin—leader of the Russian Revolution. Born in 1870, Lenin became a revolutionary while still in his teens. After taking over the leadership of the Soviet state in 1917, he instituted harsh measures to stamp out opposition. His goals included the establishment of Communist governments throughout the world and the abolition of private property. An attempt on his life in 1918 and several subsequent strokes weakened Lenin's ability to govern. He died in 1924, and the government ordered his body to be preserved. His embalmed remains are on view in a huge above-ground tomb in Red Square.

A one-ruble silver coin issued in 1924 carries several Communist symbols. On the front (left), the image of embracing workers suggests the unity of urban and rural laborers. The back of the coin (right) shows the Soviet coat of arms. Around the rim are the words "Proletarians (workers) of all lands unite."

had encouraged other European powers to prepare for war. Even after Hitler's invasion of Poland brought France and Britain into a world war against Germany in 1939, the USSR continued its policy of avoiding conflict with Hitler.

During this period, the Soviet Union invaded Finland to force the small nation to surrender land to the Soviets for military bases. In 1940 the USSR annexed the Baltic republics of Lithuania, Latvia, and Estonia. (Many countries, including the United States, have yet to recognize the Baltic States as part of the USSR.)

Despite the nonaggression pact, Hitler's forces attacked the Soviet Union on June 22, 1941. Hitler planned to take over the USSR's valuable oil deposits and wheat fields. The Soviets entered the conflict they call the Great Patriotic War (World War II). To defeat Germany, the Soviet state allied itself with the United States and Great Britain.

Kiev fell as the German armies overran most of the Ukraine and Byelorussia. By November 1941, Leningrad was surrounded. During a 29-month siege, about three million people in Leningrad withstood attacks and dwindling food supplies, and nearly one million civilians died.

Soviet military resistance saved Moscow, but the city of Stalingrad (now called Volgograd) was destroyed between 1942 and 1943. Nevertheless, the battle for Stalingrad signaled the turning point of the Soviet war effort. Nearly 330,000 German troops surrendered at Stalingrad, and the Soviet forces went on to push through southeastern Europe.

On May 2, 1945, the Soviets marched into Berlin, the German capital city, and —along with their Western allies—accepted Germany's official surrender five days later. The Soviet victory took a heavy toll—more than 20 million Soviet soldiers and civilians died during the Great Patriotic War. Throughout the nation, monuments testify to the country's losses of people and property.

Independent Picture Service

Josef Stalin succeeded Lenin as head of the Soviet state. His harsh dictatorship—including purges, or eliminations, of critics—robbed the USSR of many talented soldiers, scientists, writers, and teachers.

Courtesy of Brigita Barobs

A monument in Riga, the capital of the Latvian republic, commemorates the era of Latvian independence between World Wars I and II. In 1940 the Soviet government annexed Latvia, Lithuania, and Estonia, forcing them to become part of the Soviet Union.

Courtesy of National Archives

Soviet soldiers creep through a trench during the battle to save Stalingrad (now Volgograd) in late 1942. For months, Germans and Soviets fought hand to hand in the city's bombed-out streets. Although lacking supplies, the German army tried to hold on through the Soviet winter. By February 1943, however, the Germans had surrendered.

Courtesy of Professor Tom Muir Wilson

Veterans of World War II proudly display their military medals in Red Square.

POSTWAR GAINS

Although the European phase of World War II was over, the Asian phase continued. The USSR did not declare war on Japan until August 8, 1945, although its allies had been fighting the Japanese since 1941. Less than a month after entering the war, Soviet forces had gone deeply into Korea and northeastern China. The combined Allied efforts caused Japan to surrender on September 2, 1945. As a result of Allied agreements, the USSR gained the Kuril Islands and the southern half of Sakhalin Island from Japan. In Europe, the Soviets also increased the land areas of the Ukraine and Byelorussia at the expense of Poland and Czechoslovakia.

After the war, Soviet troops remained in Eastern Europe. Soviet leaders directed the adoption of the Communist system in Poland, Czechoslovakia, Bulgaria, Romania, Hungary, and East Germany. These states became "satellite" countries—that is, they were under Soviet influence but were not part of the USSR.

The Cold War

At the end of World War II, the USSR and the United States emerged as the two leading world powers. Their wartime cooperation soon began to cool, however, and finally deteriorated into a cold war (a political and economic rivalry short of armed conflict).

The Cold War pitted the capitalist United States and its allies against the Communist USSR and its satellite countries. Western governments worried when the Soviet Union claimed influence over Eastern Europe in the 1940s and when China adopted a Communist form of government in 1949. The Soviet Union was equally afraid of the intentions of Western powers. This fear was further aroused when the United States built military bases in Europe and Asia.

The Korean War (1950–1953) resulted from these concerns. Soviet-supplied soldiers from Communist China and North Korea fought against United Nations troops, made up primarily of U.S. forces, in South Korea. A truce ended this "hot" conflict in the Cold War in 1953.

A period of shared leadership of the USSR followed Stalin's death in 1953. Eventually, Nikita Khrushchev, the Communist party chief, assumed control of the Soviet Union. Khrushchev wanted to strengthen the Soviet economy, to increase the Communist party's control over the Soviet Union, and to encourage Communism abroad.

THE KHRUSHCHEV YEARS

Khrushchev began an era of relaxed conditions, including a "de-Stalinization" campaign that rejected Stalin's harsh policies and practices. Khrushchev also revised traditional Communist theory to permit the Soviet Union to live in peace with nations having different political systems. This change offended China's Communist regime and began a gradual decline in the relationship between the Soviet Union and China.

Under Khrushchev, Soviet scientists sent the world's first artificial satellite—

Courtesy of United Nations

Nikita Khrushchev, leader of the USSR between 1958 and 1964, used international public forums – such as the United Nations – to spread his views.

called Sputnik I—into space in 1957 and followed it with space journeys by human beings. Although Khrushchev supported limitations on military arms, Soviet technological advances included the making of

MRBM LAUNCH SITE 3
SAN CRISTOBAL, CUBA
27 OCTOBER 1962

LAUNCH AREA

NUCLEAR WARHEAD BUNKER U/C

PERMANENT BLDGS

Courtesy of John Fitzgerald Kennedy Library

In 1962 the Soviet Union and the United States nearly clashed over Soviet missiles placed on the Caribbean island of Cuba. This aerial photograph shows one of the launch sites in western Cuba.

Leonid Brezhnev took over from Khrushchev as head of the Communist party in 1964. The new leader strengthened the Soviet army and encouraged trade with Western nations.

Khrushchev made progress on the international front, but his policies at home failed. Harvests declined, industrial productivity decreased, and consumer goods made in state-owned factories were both of inferior quality and in short supply.

In 1962 Soviet placement of nuclear missiles in Cuba almost led to war with the United States. Diplomatic communications and a U.S. blockade of Cuba resolved the Cuban Missile Crisis. But Soviet leaders became convinced that Khrushchev was pursuing policies that threatened Soviet security and prestige. In 1964 Leonid Brezhnev replaced Khrushchev as head of the Communist party.

Brezhnev's Era

Brezhnev cracked down on Soviets who spoke out for basic human rights. He also restricted artistic and cultural activities. In addition, the Soviet Union exerted its authority over Eastern Europe. In 1968—when the Czechoslovakian Communist party tried to establish a different style of Communism—the Soviets sent troops into Czechoslovakia and replaced the government's leaders.

atomic bombs, which the United States also had developed. The Soviet Union and the United States began to compete with each other for superiority in nuclear weaponry.

Three Soviet soldiers parade in Red Square. During Brezhnev's years in power, the USSR sent troops to many countries to support Communist movements. In Afghanistan, for example, Soviet forces and weaponry arrived in 1979 to prop up a weak Communist regime.

In time, however, the Soviet Union realized that it needed Western machinery and food products to satisfy consumer demands. Improved relations between the United States and China encouraged the Soviet Union to strengthen its ties to the United States and Western Europe. This period, called détente (relaxation of tensions), began in the early 1970s. It reached a high point when successive U.S. presidents visited the Soviet Union during the rest of the decade.

Within the nation, Brezhnev failed to solve the Soviet Union's severe economic problems. Financial planning continued to emphasize heavy industry. The nation consistently fell behind in basic technology, and consumer products remained in short supply. Several poor harvests during the 1970s forced the Soviet Union to import grain.

By 1980 Brezhnev's poor health created many difficulties for Soviet decision makers. Without strong leadership, the government drifted from one policy to another. When Brezhnev died in 1982, Soviet citizens hoped for fresh, active leadership.

New Leaders

Yuri Andropov, head of the Soviet secret police (called the KGB), succeeded Brezhnev. But health problems caused his death at age 69 in January 1984. Because reformers and old-style party bureaucrats could not agree on who should succeed Andropov, a compromise candidate, Konstantin Chernenko, was chosen. Chernenko, aged 73, died in March 1985. Reform-minded Mikhail Gorbachev replaced him at the age of 54.

Gorbachev represents a new generation of Soviet leaders. The two key ideas of his administration have been *glasnost* (openness) and *perestroika* (restructuring). Both words imply a change of Soviet policy.

Glasnost preserves the Communist monopoly of power but encourages party members to openly discuss issues that af-

Photo by UPI/Bettmann Newsphotos

Soviet leader Mikhail Gorbachev and his wife, Raisa, have promoted the image of *glasnost* (openness) during trips abroad. Here, they greet newspeople in New York City before a reception in their honor.

fect the development of the country. The new policy allows Soviets more freedom to discuss politics, to report news, to write history, and to produce films.

In the workplace, openness has resulted in worker-management cooperation and in greater support for economic ideas generated by individuals. In the realm of foreign relations, glasnost has led Gorbachev to explore a new relationship with the United States and other nations. Recent agreements—including the 1987 Intermediate-range Nuclear Forces (INF) Treaty—have reduced the buildup of nuclear weapons in the two countries.

Perestroika addresses the restructuring of the Soviet economic system, which has produced neither well-made nor sufficient consumer goods. The policy is intended to foster productivity and efficiency in the industrial sector. Soviet leaders have also encouraged private production, especially on farms, to increase the amount and quality of consumer goods.

Private and cooperative stores, factories, and restaurants are now legal in the Soviet Union. For the first time, a profit motive—working for personal gain (as opposed to striving for a shared goal)—appears among worker ideals. The Soviet government also is encouraging foreign companies and banks to invest in the USSR.

Recent Events

In late 1988, Gorbachev reorganized the Communist party and replaced many old-style politicians who had been thwarting his reforms. In addition to streamlining the administration, Gorbachev took on the formerly ceremonial job of president of the Presidium (permanent executive committee) of the Supreme Soviet. He made the presidency an active post with greater power. The president's aim is to revitalize the Soviet economy, in part to answer the demands of its increasingly dissatisfied citizens.

In the late 1980s, several ethnic republics—including Armenia, Azerbaijan, Kazakhstan, and the Baltic States—participated, sometimes violently, in nationalist demonstrations and political rallies. Some of the protests were aimed at changing long-standing boundaries that have cut through ethnic communities. Other unrest has emphasized the dissatisfaction of minority populations with predominantly Russian rule. The Soviet Union's Eastern European allies also attempted to make more decisions without Soviet influence. Complex questions face the new leadership as it seeks to firmly establish glasnost and perestroika within the USSR and perhaps throughout the Soviet sphere of influence.

Government

The formal Soviet government has executive, legislative, and judicial branches whose authority is based on a constitution. The present constitution, adopted in 1977, is a revision of earlier documents. The Soviet constitution provides for individual

In Tallinn, the capital of Estonia, a 1988 poster reveals the negative reaction of some of the city's residents to being part of the USSR. The cartoon shows Josef Stalin, like the Pied Piper, leading three children labeled Lithuania, Latvia, and Estonia with his tune on the virtues of Communism. Backing up Stalin is a tough soldier tagged as Russian military power. In 1988 Estonia asserted its right to reject Soviet laws that limit local authority. The Soviet government declared the Estonian decision invalid.

"PLAYING 'FOLLOW THE LEADER'"

rights, but historically these freedoms have been denied to ordinary Soviet citizens. For example, freedom of speech and of political action are guaranteed but must not be anti-Communist in nature.

A recent reorganization plan established a directly elected, part-time legislature called the Congress of People's Deputies. This body, in turn, chooses the members of the Supreme Soviet, which has authority over some legislative activities. Headed by a president, the Supreme Soviet and its Council of Ministers are important legislative subunits. In theory, the Supreme Soviet is independent. In practice, however, it approves the policies put forward by the Communist party. High-ranking people in the party usually dominate the Supreme Soviet and the council. Elections held in 1989 broadened the membership of these legislative bodies.

The Soviet court system operates according to the ideals of the Communist party. The judicial system often has been used to suppress opposition to Soviet views. Many dissidents (those who dis-agree with Soviet policy) have been imprisoned or have had their activities restricted according to Soviet laws.

THE COMMUNIST PARTY

The Communist party of the Soviet Union is the only legal political party in the country, and its leader is usually the most powerful person in the Soviet Union. Every four years a party congress convenes and elects the members of a central committee to run the party between congress meetings. Major Soviet policies originate in the Central Committee, which instructs the government, the military, and civilian organizations on issues that affect most aspects of Soviet life.

In turn, the Central Committee elects the members of two bodies—the Politburo and the Secretariat—to direct its affairs between meetings. The Politburo is composed of about a dozen high-ranking Soviet Communists who develop party policy. The Secretariat—the party's chief executive arm—is responsible for the party's day-to-day administration.

Within the Kremlin in Moscow are many government buildings. The Communist party uses the Palace of Congresses for its meetings. When not needed for political purposes, the large hall hosts ballet and opera performances.

A mother adjusts her child's winter clothing. Most Soviet women choose to have small families, in part because they work full-time and because urban housing for large families is scarce. Despite a low birthrate, birth control methods are not widely used, and state-funded abortions are common.

3) The People

In 1990 the population of the Soviet Union was about 291 million, and two-thirds of the inhabitants lived in urban areas. Over 70 percent of the people resided in Soviet Europe, and the rest made their homes in Soviet Asia.

Despite Communist ideals that proclaim the equality of all people, the USSR is still a layered society. The state no longer gives special privileges to the landed aristocracy and the wealthy, as in tsarist days. It does, however, bestow preferred status on government officials, star athletes, famous musicians, and cosmonauts (Soviet astronauts). Ordinary citizens wait in long lines to buy scarce meat, fresh bread, and other necessities. The elite go to special stores, where most items are in stock.

An Uzbek man wears a traditional embroidered skullcap at a market in the southwestern Soviet Union.

Ethnic Mixture

Because the huge nation is composed of 15 distinct republics, the ethnic mixture of the Soviet Union is extremely diverse and includes as many as 100 nationalities. This varied culture may be roughly divided into people of Slavic, Turkic, and other backgrounds.

The Slavs make up about 75 percent of the total population. More than 50 percent of the Slavs are Russians, who dominate the governmental and Communist party leadership. Other Slavic groups include the Ukrainians and the Byelorussians.

After the Slavs, the Turkic peoples—who live mostly in central Asia—are the country's largest ethnic group. The biggest Turkic community is the Uzbek. They are followed in size by the Kazakhs, the Azerbaijani, and the Turkmen.

Other groups that do not share common languages with Slavic or Turkic people live

Georgian actors perform in a television production of *Don Quixote* in Tbilisi, the capital of the Georgian Soviet Socialist Republic (S.S.R.). Television and radio are important media for keeping alive minority languages, such as Georgian.

mostly in Soviet Europe. Speakers of Indo-European languages include Lithuanians and Latvians, who dwell near the Baltic Sea. Moldavians, who are related to Romanians, and Armenians, who reside in the Caucasus Mountains, also belong to the Indo-European group.

Jews—whom the Soviet government considers a nationality rather than a religious group—are scattered in urban centers throughout the Soviet Union. The Estonians, who are ethnically related to the Finns, reside in the Baltic region. They speak a language that is not related to the tongues used in other Baltic States. Georgians—members of yet another nationality—live in the region of the Caucasus Mountains.

Education

After the fall of the Russian Empire, the new Soviet state put great emphasis on ed-

ucation. The government wanted not only to increase literacy but also to promote Marxist and Communist ideals among a new generation of students. In 1990 nearly everyone in the Soviet Union could read and write.

The Soviet government requires all pupils to finish 10 years of school between the ages of 7 and 17. The state funds all schools in the USSR, and the Communist party approves the course of studies at every level. Government scholarships support students in secondary and postsecondary institutions. If students excel in their work, they receive 25 percent more than the regular stipend.

Basic academic skills are emphasized at the elementary level, and science and higher mathematics are introduced in the middle grades. Secondary schools focus either on the sciences or on industrial skills. Students must also take courses in Marxist-Leninist theories. After school, most

SOVIET UNION
REPUBLICS AND SELECTED ADMINISTRATIVE UNITS

Artwork by Carol F. Barrett

At a collective farm school in Kiev, pupils use calculators in their coursework. Math and science are heavily emphasized at the middle and secondary levels. Good grades can assure a Soviet student of a place at a university and a promising career.

students are required to clean and repair their school's grounds and buildings. Music, sports, and crafts are also after-school activities.

Health

Free, universal health care was a priority of the Soviet state in the 1920s. Since then, the number of doctors, other medical personnel, hospitals, and clinics has steadily risen, and patients pay little for medical services.

Unsafe water continues to be a health hazard in rural areas, where sanitation facilities sometimes are poor. But instances of water-carried diseases—such as cholera—have declined. In recent years, the major causes of death in the USSR have been cancer and heart disease.

The Soviet government emphasizes good health care for mothers and babies, including pre- and post-birth examinations. The state also funds government-run nurseries for working mothers and children's

clinics. Yet, overall health care in the USSR sometimes is below the standard for developed countries.

In 1990 the life expectancy for Soviet citizens was 69 years, compared to 74 for other industrialized countries. In the Soviet Union, 29 babies out of every 1,000 die before they are one year old. In other developed nations, the ratio is 16 out of 1,000. Some of these differences result from shortages of medicines in the USSR.

Language and Literature

More than 100 languages are spoken in the Soviet Union. They belong to many different families and are written in various alphabets. Russian, Byelorussian, Ukrainian, Latvian, Lithuanian, and Armenian are Indo-European tongues. Uzbek and Azerbaijani resemble Turkish. Estonian and several secondary languages are related to Finnish. In addition, many smaller groupings exist, such as the Caucasian family, which includes Georgian.

This graph compares health statistics in the Soviet Union with those in other developed countries of the world. About three-fourths of all Soviet doctors are women, and medical services are free and readily available. (Data from the Population Reference Bureau, Washington, D.C.)

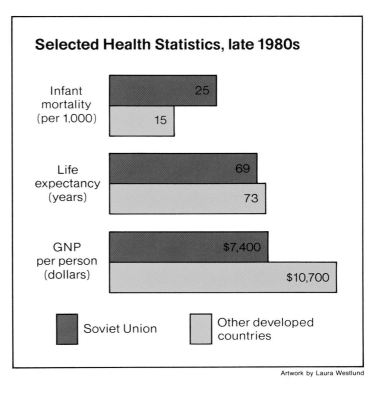

Selected Health Statistics, late 1980s

Infant mortality (per 1,000)
- Soviet Union: 25
- Other developed countries: 15

Life expectancy (years)
- Soviet Union: 69
- Other developed countries: 73

GNP per person (dollars)
- Soviet Union: $7,400
- Other developed countries: $10,700

■ Soviet Union   □ Other developed countries

Artwork by Laura Westlund

Courtesy of Steve Feinstein

A sign in the Cyrillic alphabet—in which Russian and other national languages are written—advertises Pepsi in Moscow. The Soviet government allowed the soft drink to be sold in the USSR in the 1970s.

Most Soviet people use the Cyrillic alphabet, in which Russian—the official language of the USSR—is written. Latvian, Lithuanian, and Estonian, however, appear in the Latin alphabet. The Georgian, Armenian, and Turkic languages have ancient alphabets of their own, which are different from the Latin and Cyrillic written forms. Modern Turkic languages, however, are now written in Cyrillic.

Most early Russian literary works appeared in Old Slavonic, the language of the Russian Orthodox Church. Later authors of the imperial era introduced more common forms of Russian in their works.

The nineteenth-century poet Alexander Pushkin used strong word images to enliven his verse. His creative output includes *Boris Godunov,* Russia's first national drama, and *Eugene Onegin,* one of the world's great narrative poems. Fyodor Dostoyevsky, who followed Pushkin, produced works that explore human psychology. Among his best-known books are *The Brothers Karamazov* and *Crime and Punishment.* The epic novels of Leo Tolstoy—such as *War and Peace* and *Anna Karenina*—show the author's insight into the human mind. The late nineteenth-century short stories and plays of Anton Chekhov also enjoy great popularity.

The Russian Revolution of 1917 produced a new literary guideline called socialist realism. According to this principle, literature and art had to conform to Communist ideals. The style of the work had to be realistic, not symbolic; its content had to be socialist. Maxim Gorky and Aleksei Tolstoy were among the early supporters of the government's new approach to writing and art. Some authors, however, refused to accept socialist realism's restrictions. Boris Pasternak and Alexander Solzhenitsyn, for example, wrote books that revealed some of the deficiencies and excesses of Soviet life. As a result, their books were banned in the USSR, but both writers were awarded the international Nobel Prize for literature.

Independent Picture Service

Born in Moscow in 1799, Alexander Pushkin became Russia's leading poet while still in his twenties. Known for his long poems that tell an involved story, Pushkin also wrote short stories and plays. He died in 1837 from wounds inflicted during a duel with a Frenchman who admired his wife.

Independent Picture Service

Maxim Gorky *(shown carrying his son)* grew up in the last years of the Russian Empire. His early works criticized the state's efforts to curb human freedom, and he eventually supported Lenin and the Communist party. Gorky's play *The Lower Depths* and his novel *The Mother* describe the misery of ordinary Russians under tsarist rule.

48

Courtesy of Harper and Row, Publishers, Inc.

In 1970 the Soviet writer Alexander Solzhenitsyn was awarded the Nobel Prize for literature. Within his own country, however, Solzhenitsyn's works were regarded as attacks on the government. In his trilogy, *The Gulag Archipelago,* Solzhenitsyn wrote about Soviet prison camps, where people accused of political crimes were sent. The government took away Solzhenitsyn's citizenship and banished him from the country in 1974.

Courtesy of Minneapolis Public Library and Information Center

St. Basil's Cathedral was built in the mid-sixteenth century to commemorate Ivan the Terrible's conquest of the city of Kazan in the west central USSR. The structure, which is now a museum, actually consists of nine churches connected by elevated walkways. Colorful tiles and ornate patterns distinguish each of the cathedral's towers.

Religion

When the Communists came to power, they wanted to destroy the influence of the Russian Orthodox Church. As a result, the new regime strongly supported atheism—a view that denies the existence of a divine being. Nevertheless, many Soviets still practice a religion.

The largest religious denomination in the USSR is the Russian Orthodox Church, although Armenian and Georgian Orthodox churches also exist. Supporters of Islam, called Muslims, are the next largest group, and they live mostly in central Asia.

Roman Catholics, Lutherans, Baptist-Evangelicals, Jews, and Buddhists make up much of the rest of the religious population. Roman Catholics are largely from the Lithuanian republic, and Lutherans reside particularly in Latvia and Estonia. Baptist-Evangelicals are one of the few religious groups recognized by the Soviet state, principally because they initially accepted Soviet ideas. Buddhists—who follow a philosophy developed in India in the sixth century B.C.—practice in many Asian parts of the Soviet Union.

The Soviet Union contains about two million Jews. The government has put more limitations on Jews than it has on Christians and Muslims. For example, Jews—unlike other minorities in the Soviet Union—are not allowed to use their own languages, principally Yiddish and Hebrew. The USSR has also persistently pursued anti-Jewish policies that make it difficult for Jews to publish, to worship, or to succeed in their careers. As a result, many Jews have tried to leave the country. Gorbachev's policies, however, may improve the position of Soviet Jews.

Although many churches and places of worship have been open to the public for decades, most of the people who attend are older men and women. Members of the clergy depend on their own sources of income or on donations from their congregations to make a living.

Although the Soviet government discourages religious ceremonies, many traditional celebrations still occur. Here, faithful Georgian Orthodox Christians gather at an Easter vigil.

A prayer in Aramaic – a Semitic language similar to Hebrew and Arabic – appears in a Jewish synagogue in Tbilisi.

The state strictly limits the amount of religious teaching the clergy may do. Consequently, younger Soviets have not had much spiritual education and know little about religion. Important Christian holidays—such as Easter and Christmas—draw large crowds. In 1988 Gorbachev eased restrictions on organized religions and encouraged the restoration of many churches and monasteries.

Art and Music

Although folk arts once flourished in many parts of Russia, the introduction of Christianity in the tenth century changed Russian art forms. Icons—heavily symbolic religious pictures—are strongly represented in early Russian painting. This religious emphasis extended to architecture, which developed a distinctly Russian church style that featured onion-shaped domes, carved doorways, and patterned exteriors.

In the eighteenth century, when Western influences on Russia increased, European themes appeared in Russian paintings. Artists of the nineteenth century tended to depict ordinary country life, sometimes in a critical way.

After the Russian Revolution, the state determined artistic modes. The regime favored socialist realism as a means of producing artworks that praised the goals and achievements of Communism. To a great extent, modern Soviet artists retain this style, although a strong nonconformist artistic movement exists. Its supporters—who often do not follow established Soviet guidelines—sometimes produce works that criticize the state.

Music has also changed from one historical period to the next. By the nineteenth century, Russian musicians employed Western forms. Mikhail Glinka wrote operas based on national themes. Composers such as Nikolai Rimsky-Korsakov and Peter Ilich Tchaikovsky produced orchestral and chamber music. These works were often based on Russian folk songs.

Courtesy of Elvehjem Museum of Art, University of Wisconsin-Madison, Gift of Joseph E. Davies, Ambassador to Russia

This sixteenth-century Russian icon, or religious painting, depicts scenes from the birth of Jesus. Artists who produce icons follow age-old traditions of painting and symbolism, which are contained in the *Podlinnik,* or painter's handbook.

Courtesy of Minneapolis Public Library and Information Center

Born in Moscow in 1866, Wassily Kandinsky helped to found the abstract movement, which does not use figures in its art. His earlier works, such as *Sunday (Old Russia)* (above), use thick dabs of paint to create a glimmering mosaic of color. After years of study in Europe, Kandinsky returned to Russia in 1914. Until late 1921, he taught in Moscow, where he established the Russian Academy of Artistic Sciences. He left Russia in 1921 and eventually settled in France, where he died in 1944.

Independent Picture Service

An oil painting produced in the 1950s depicts Lenin addressing an enthusiastic crowd. In keeping with the guidelines of socialist realism, the work supports the socialist movement and realistically portrays its subject matter.

Courtesy of Marion Moore

In the late 1980s, the Soviet government allowed Western musicians—including Billy Joel, James Taylor, and Ray Charles—to perform in the USSR. Here, the Minnesota-based group Women Who Cook! sings to an audience in Sochi, a resort town on the Black Sea.

Independent Picture Service

Peter Ilich Tchaikovsky, the first Russian composer to become internationally famous, studied music in St. Petersburg and later taught in Moscow. His greatest works—including the ballets *Swan Lake* and *The Nutcracker*—appeared between 1875 and the early 1890s.

When the Communists took power in 1917, many Russian musicians left the country permanently. Those who remained or returned—including Dimitri Shostakovich and Sergei Prokofiev—produced works within the guidelines demanded by the state.

Beginning in the 1950s, a new interest in Western music—principally jazz and rock compositions—arose. Although the state long regarded Western music as destructive to Communist ideals, the government has relaxed its views somewhat in recent years. Jazz and rock records are now more accessible, and the government has allowed U.S. and Western European performers to appear in major cities.

Sports

Encouraged by their government—which provides many sports facilities—Soviet citizens enthusiastically support a variety of competitive activities. The people participate as either athletes or as spectators. Although professional sports are not officially permitted in the USSR, the government pays gifted athletes. The most popular sport is soccer, and both young and old people fill the stadiums during a match. Basketball, hockey, and chess follow soccer as favorite pastimes.

Since 1952, Soviet athletes have participated in the Olympic Games, and the nation sponsored the twenty-second Olympiad in Moscow in 1980. In international competition, Soviet athletes excel in gymnastics, ice skating, weight lifting, and hockey.

Photo by Stan Waldhauser

Young and old Soviets play chess—in parks, at home, and at school. Within the USSR, chess is regarded not merely as a game of skill but as an important part of Soviet culture. Tournaments are organized at all playing levels, and chess grand masters often receive high national honors.

Long lines are evidence of the USSR's shortage of basic foodstuffs and consumer items. These Muscovites (residents of Moscow) wait at a shop on Kalinin Prospekt (street) in the hope of buying sausages.

4) The Economy

Since 1928, the Soviet economy has been carefully regimented by five-year plans, which guide managers in deciding where to concentrate resources and workers. The first three five-year plans focused on the development of heavy industry and on the search for raw materials. As a result, industry experienced remarkable growth in a short timespan.

Since the 1950s, the five-year plans have stressed increases in consumer goods, housing, and agricultural items. In the 1970s—after decades of failing to reach the government's quotas—the economy slowed down, and the quality of consumer goods declined. Modernization of industrial methods did not produce the increased output that Soviet planners had expected. Consumers waited for years to purchase cars and refrigerators. When the goods finally were available, they were often of poor quality.

In the late 1980s, production shortages and the inferiority of Soviet goods raised important questions about the means of production. The USSR began to fall behind in areas that involved complex technology, such as computer hardware and scientific equipment.

To encourage initiative and to raise the quality of technology and goods, Gorbachev has allowed greater freedom in the Soviet economy. Under new laws, individuals can establish their own businesses.

They can also sell what they make at markets in which the government does not set the prices. State-run farms now have more flexibility in planning their crops, and industrial firms are encouraged to improve quality and productivity. Because of Gorbachev's reforms, foreign investors, including countries from the West, are becoming interested in the USSR.

Industry

Nearly 40 percent of the Soviet Union's gross national product (the value of goods and services produced in a year) come from the industrial sector. The nation's main output is in heavy industry, and the USSR provides 20 percent of the world's industrial products, including vehicles and weaponry.

The Soviet economy has devoted much of its budget to the production of sophisticated weaponry – such as this missile launcher – at the expense of making ordinary products. Recent improvements in Soviet economic and military planning are changing this emphasis.

A statue honoring rural and urban workers suggests the value placed on manual labor in the USSR.

The Soviet government strictly controls manufacturing, deciding how many items to produce and where to sell them. Moscow leads all Soviet urban centers in industrial production. The capital's factories mainly make autos, trucks, and buses, and smaller firms turn out electronic equipment, textiles, chemicals, and processed food. Shipbuilding is a big industry in the port of Leningrad, and the Ukraine produces iron and steel. More factories are being built in Siberia, where vast fuel resources are available to power manufacturing plants.

Gorbachev's reforms have changed the management of Soviet industry. A greater emphasis is now placed on high-quality production, and accounting methods have become strict. As a result of higher standards, Soviet managers can now fire unproductive laborers who do not meet factory needs.

Workers pack clothing in boxes at a factory in suburban Moscow. The garment sector of the textile industry has grown, but styles often lag behind those in other countries.

This 1988 Lada—a compact, two-door vehicle—was made in Tolyatti, an auto center on the Volga River. Soviet assembly plants build most of the autos driven in the USSR.

Soviet laborers in Leningrad wind a stationary set of blades around a turbogenerator. This energy-producing machine can be used to pump water, to supply electricity, or to propel jet engines.

An alternative to state-owned industries has appeared in the growth of cooperative organizations. Workers get together to produce a particular consumer item and pay themselves wages based on sales. Some of these organizations have been remarkably successful.

Much of industrial production and trade in the Soviet Union is connected to what is called the black market. Black marketers sell goods from private factories, as well as products coming from outside the Soviet Union. The success of this underground economy is tied to the desire of many Soviet citizens to acquire goods—such as jeans, leather jackets, and musical tapes—from the West. Often these products, as well as locally published books, are only available at very high prices.

Agriculture

Collective farms—a form of shared agriculture—originated in 1928 with the USSR's first five-year plan. The government owned all of the land, and farmers worked together to plant and harvest the crops. Under this system, the workers shared the ownership of farm buildings, livestock, and farm machinery.

In recent years, Soviet agriculture has suffered setbacks, partly because of harsh weather conditions and the farmers' lack of motivation to produce food. Poor harvests have forced the government to buy enormous quantities of grain from foreign countries, particularly the United States and Canada. Agricultural problems include shortages of modern machinery and chemical fertilizers.

Courtesy of Russell Adams

Throughout the Soviet Union, collective farmers' markets offer surplus produce for sale. Many foodstuffs, however, are scarce, and often only a small variety of fresh food is available at one time.

A combine harvests a field of wheat in Irkutsk, near Lake Baikal in the southern USSR. Wheat volumes have sometimes dropped in recent years, causing the Soviet government to import the grain from Canada and the United States.

A collective farm worker proudly displays ripe cucumbers at a huge greenhouse in Kiev. She receives low wages but also gets a share in the profits of the farm. In contrast, state farms are run like factories, and laborers are paid a straight wage.

Changes in working conditions in the late 1980s aimed to overcome these drawbacks. But progress has been slow. The most visible of the agricultural reforms permits collective farmers to sell surplus crops on the open market and to keep the money that these crops generate. Gorbachev has even suggested that the collective farm system be dismantled.

Although the Soviet Union has vast amounts of farmable land, much of it lies in cold areas where the growing season is short. Cereal grains such as barley, rye, and wheat are major crops. Barley is grown all over the country, and rye is often planted in the wetter parts of Soviet Europe. The Ukraine, Siberia, and Kazakhstan are the main wheat-producing areas.

The USSR is also a leading producer of apples, potatoes, and sugar beets. With irrigation, cotton thrives in central Asia, and tea plants flourish near the Black Sea. Livestock raising has increased only gradually—which accounts for some of the meat shortages throughout the country. The Ukraine has beef and dairy cattle, and sheep graze on the steppes of central Asia.

Courtesy of Russell Adams

Sheep graze on a grassy hillside in Stavropol Krai, a territory in the southwestern Russian republic. State farms raise more sheep than collective farms do.

Forestry and Fishing

The Soviet Union is the world's largest producer of lumber, particularly pine and larch. Birch is the principal hardwood harvested in Soviet forests. Much of the

Photo by Kathryn W. Holland

Buyers and sellers—many of them dressed in traditional Turkic clothing—bargain over fruit and fowl at an open-air market in Samarkand. Nestled in a fertile valley in the Uzbek S.S.R., farms near Samarkand produce a variety of foodstuffs. The city also has a long history as a center of Islamic learning.

forest industry is located in Soviet Europe, whose woodlands are accessible. Siberia has far greater resources of wood, but transportation problems make the trees hard to ship to export centers.

Because meat is scarce, fish is an important source of protein in the Soviet diet. The Soviet government has expanded the nation's fishing fleet, which now travels beyond coastal waters into international oceans and seas. Fishing crews bring in catches of herring, salmon, and cod, and some fishermen prey on endangered species such as whales, walrus, and seals. Black Sea sturgeon are valuable because their eggs can be processed into caviar—a salty delicacy that brings in large amounts of export income.

Mining and Energy

The USSR has large natural gas reserves, as well as substantial deposits of minerals and oil. These metals and fuels lie mainly in the Urals, the Ukraine, and Siberia. The nation leads the world in the extraction of iron ore, natural gas, nickel, and petroleum. Also of importance are mines that produce gold, zinc, coal, copper, and silver.

The Soviet Union ranks high in the production of electricity, often tapping the power of its many rivers. Until recently, coal was the main source of fuel in the Soviet Union. Because oil and natural gas are far more convenient to use, however, the USSR is now emphasizing the development of these energy sources.

A tractor pulls a load of cut timber through the snows of Soviet Europe. Although far more forests exist in Soviet Asia, the Asian trees are hard to reach, are thinner in girth, and take a longer time to mature because of harsh weather.

Fishermen add another netful to their day's catch in the Baikal region. Canned seafood is a growing part of the Soviet economy.

Onshore oil rigs are found in many parts of the Soviet Union. The nation's underground petroleum reserves are thought to rival those of the entire Middle East.

Nuclear power also figures into the USSR's energy network. In April 1986 one of its nuclear power stations caught fire, releasing large amounts of radioactivity into the air. The government admitted that human error caused the explosion at the Chernobyl power plant. The Soviets received outside help to deal with the fire and health emergencies that resulted from the disaster.

Transportation

Railways dominate the Soviet Union's transportation channels. The track carries

Only months before it caught fire in a nuclear disaster, the Chernobyl power plant was photographed for a Soviet magazine. Located near Kiev, the plant emitted dangerous levels of radiation when a hydrogen explosion destroyed the nuclear reactor. Winds carried the radiation throughout Europe, contaminating farm vegetables and food for livestock as far away as Scotland.

61

In urban areas, trams are a common form of transportation. Many cities are developing subways to ease traffic congestion.

about 50 percent of the nation's freight and 40 percent of its passengers. Almost 90,000 miles of track connect the country, including a rail line that runs from Moscow to Vladivostok on the Pacific Ocean—a distance of 5,600 miles.

Roads cover about 500,000 miles of Soviet territory and provide travel routes for the nation's 10 million motorists. Cars are not readily available in the USSR. Buyers have to wait many years to get an automobile. The purchase can absorb as much as six years' pay.

Aeroflot—the national airline of the Soviet Union—links all of the country's major cities. The airline also handles international traffic, mostly through Moscow's three large airports.

Aeroflot is responsible for domestic and international air services in the USSR. The huge distances to be covered—as well as winter conditions that prevent overland travel—encourage the extensive use of airplanes as a means of getting from place to place.

The Future

With a new leader in 1985, the Soviet Union began a fresh era in its history. Mikhail Gorbachev's reforms aim to make the USSR a more open society, as well as one that is better managed and more productive. Many of Gorbachev's colleagues in the Communist party disagree with his new approach. They believe that a higher level of freedom will undermine the Communist party's national control as well as their own power. Gorbachev's reorganization of the government in late 1988 removed many of his most vocal opponents.

Future results of the new policies may include a worldwide decrease in nuclear weaponry and greater respect for traditional human rights within the USSR. The government has extended unfamiliar freedoms and is listening to views that disagree with national policy. Gorbachev's goals—to revitalize the Soviet Union and to give its citizens a better quality of life—are clear. Whether he will be able or allowed to achieve them remains uncertain.

Courtesy of Brigita Barobs

In August 1988, during a demonstration in Tallinn, Estonia, protesters displayed signs to free a local political activist.

Courtesy of Steve Feinstein

Members of the Young Octobrists—a Communist organization that arranges after-school activities for students under age 10—pose during a visit to Red Square. After being an Octobrist, a young Soviet may become a Pioneer and later a member of the Young Communist League. These organizations play important educational roles and also instill national ideals in new generations of Soviet citizens.

Index